Hello, It's Me!

(A Very Special Book About One Incredible, Wonderful, Spectacular Kid!)

By Elena Schietinger

(with a lot of help from _____)

write your name here

Archway Publishing books may be ordered through booksellers or by contacting:

Archway Publishing
1663 Liberty Drive
Bloomington, IN 47403
www.archwaypublishing.com
844-669-3957

ISBN: 978-1-6657-2413-5 (sc)
ISBN: 978-1-6657-2414-2 (hc)
ISBN: 978-1-6657-2412-8 (e)

Print information available on the last page.

Archway Publishing rev. date: 06/27/2022

A Message to the Reader

This book is special because it is about a very special person. That person is YOU! It is all about what makes you happy, and proud, and all the other feelings you feel at this very special age that you are right now. It is about where you live, and who you love, and all the things that fill up your very special days.

But, this book is also special because YOU get to help write it and illustrate it. Yes, it's true! Very special YOU get to be an author and an illustrator. On each page, you will write something about yourself and draw an awesome picture to go with what you write. Now, someone may help you with the writing, but all of the thoughts that this very special book will contain once you are done will be your own. That's what will make it truly special! And, once the book is finished, your teachers and your parents and all the other people who love you will be able to read it and learn lots of things about wonderful YOU! But most of all, when you grow older, and the wonderful age that you are right now is only a memory, this book will remind you and everyone who reads it of who you were at this very special stage of your life. And, it is something you will have forever... sort of like a photo, only more amazing because it will have been made by very special YOU!

One last thing! If you happen to be doing this for your birthday, do it again next year and every birthday after that. Then, you'll be able to see just how much you change with each passing year!

So, set yourself up with some markers or crayons and let's get going! This very special book is just waiting to get started.

This is me.

I am   years old.

This is me on my last birthday!

My birthday is

This is my family.

The members of my family are

What I like best about my family is

This is where I live.

What I like best about my home is

When I think about my
home, it makes me feel

This is my best friend, whose name is

I like my best friend because

These are the other people who love me the most in the world.

This is my school. It's called

My grade is

(Remember, preschool is a grade, too!)

This is my teacher.
My teacher's name is

My teacher makes school

This is me when I am happy.
I am happiest when

If I ever get sad, it's because

My favorite thing to do is

I don't like it when I have to

My favorite food is

My least favorite food is

My favorite color is

My favorite outfit is

I have chores! My favorite chore is

My least favorite chore is

The way I feel about chores is

This is me with my favorite toy.

This is me with the pet I have *(or the pet I WANT to have!)*.

I think the PERFECT pet name is

When I'm being funny, it looks like this.

When I'm serious, it looks like this.

I am NOT afraid of

But I am afraid of

(The people who love me tell me not to be!)

I am proud that I

I know I am helpful when I

When I go to sleep, this is what I dream about.

When I wake up each day, here is what I look forward to.

This is what I want to be when I grow up.

My one wish is

This is something I am REALLY good at!

I know I'm special because

So, how do you like me?

I like myself a lot!

*(The people who love me say
that's really important!)*

The End.

Date completed:

Printed in the United States
by Baker & Taylor Publisher Services